COMING
OF
AGE

31 Words on How to Be Wise
Beyond Your Years

Andrew A. Hall

Copyright © 2025 Andrew A. Hall

ALL RIGHTS RESERVED. No part of this book or its associated ancillary materials may be reproduced or transmitted in any form or by any means, electronic or mechanical, including photocopying, recording, or by any informational storage or retrieval system without permission from the author.

Disclaimer

The information in this book is not meant to replace the advice of a certified professional. Please consult a licensed advisor in matters relating to your personal and professional well-being, and that of your dependants, including mental, emotional, physical, financial, business, legal matters, family planning, education, and spiritual health or practices. The views and opinions expressed throughout this book are those of the author and do not necessarily reflect the views or opinions of all the agency, organization, employer, publisher, or companies associated with this material.

Since we are critically-thinking human beings, the views of the author are always subject to change or revision at any time. Please do not hold the author or the publisher to them in perpetuity. Any references to past performance may not be indicative of future results. No warranties or guarantees are expressed or implied by the publisher's choice to include any of the content in this material.

If you choose to attempt any of the methods mentioned in this book, the author and publisher advise you take full responsibility for your safety and those you influence. The author and publisher are not liable for any damages or negative consequences from any treatment, action, application, or preparation to any person reading or following the information in this book.

The author and publisher make no representations as to the accuracy, completeness, correctness, suitability, or validity of any information in the book, and neither the publisher nor the author shall be liable for any physical, psychological, emotional, financial, or commercial damages, including, but not limited to, special, incidental, consequential, or other damages to the readers of this book.

Paperback ISBN: 979-8-9989903-0-4
Hardback ISBN: 979-8-9989903-1-1
Digital ISBN: 979-8-9989903-2-8
Audiobook ISBN: 979-8-9989903-3-5

Cover Design and Interior Formatting by 100Covers.

"*When you are young, the committee of 'they' will tell you, 'You're too young.' But a day will come when they look you in the eyes and say, 'You're too old.'*"

—**Andrew A. Hall**

"The book you don't read won't help."
-Jim Rohn

I pray the truths in this book help you deal well in life

To:
_____

From:
_____

Because (and date):
_____
_____
_____
_____

Dedication

This book is dedicated to all of the young people just like I was – wise beyond your years. You are the leaders of the future and I'm honored to dedicate this book to you.

What the first reader had to say:

By Dane Kelley, 19 year old, Deans List student

More Than Just A Daily Devotional

What is the true meaning of a devotional? That's a question I have constantly asked myself. Through the years I have come to the conclusion that it must be something that has weight to it. It must be something that is valuable in knowledge, but also something that will challenge the way you think or act. The guide/devotional by Andrew A. Hall, "Coming of Age 31 Words on How To Be Wise Beyond Your Years", does exactly that! It gives you a new perspective with knowledge and experience behind it, while having an aspect of calling you to act or at least ponder on how it connects with your everyday life, thus creating a masterpiece. As a 19 year old man myself, I find that this masterpiece was very relatable with my own life. I found myself rereading and pondering on the idea of "if I only knew that sooner". I would recommend this devotional for anyone, of all ages! I would recommend that you read this 31 day Devotional all in one day, and then go back and read one a day till you go back through it. This way, you will be able to truly grasp the idea! The word Foundation, the word used for day 10 was very germane to my life. After getting out of a fairly long relationship, I see more and more that it ended before it even began. It lacked a good foundation from the start. Andrew states in this devotional, "today you are laying the foundation for tomorrow just like today you're standing on the foundation of what you built yesterday". If your foundation isn't strong or mighty then your house can't stand. For you are who you are at your core. If your core is strong then you will be strong throughout. Another great word was the word Passion. This word was used for devotional day 20. Until I read this, I never truly grasped the idea of passion. Passion is not just something for the weak hearted, passion can be described by the word suffer. If you are passionate about something then you will not stop! No matter what it is, you will suffer to achieve your goals or your dreams... These are just some of the many lessons I have learned and/or taken from this devotional. This daily devotional is nothing but a masterpiece, a guide, a piece of knowledge that will last a lifetime.

<u>What others are saying about Andrew A. Hall and his strategies!</u>

"Andrew is wise beyond his years. He is one of the most emotionally intelligent, purpose-driven people I've ever met. He's not just wise beyond his years—he's a rare combination of visionary and grounded. A natural connector with a remarkable memory, Andrew genuinely sees and values people. His integrity is unwavering, and you can trust him without hesitation. He brings optimism, curiosity, and clarity to every conversation, and he's especially gifted in conflict resolution—creating outcomes where everyone walks away better. He's a lifelong learner, always growing, and approaches life with an abundant mindset. Beyond business, Andrew is deeply multi-dimensional, with passions that enrich everyone around him. The world needs more leaders like Andrew. Coming of Age is just the beginning—his impact will be wide-reaching and lasting."

- **Kelli Calabrese,** Faith-Based Business Coach | Speaker | Empowering Entrepreneurs to Build Profitable, Purpose-Driven Businesses & Lives | 37+ Year Expert | 4x Best Selling Author

"If you're ready to take your business and life to higher levels and sustain continuous growth and improvement, then you must work with Andrew! Not only does he share high-value content, but he has the unique ability to connect on a level that instantly changes peoples lives! And, the best thing is that Andrew comes from the heart and truly cares about making a positive difference in the lives of others! Do yourself a favor and work with Andrew today! You'll be so grateful you did!"

- **James Malinchak,** Featured on ABCs Hit TV Show, "Secret Millionaire" | One of America's Leading Keynote Speakers & Business Coaches

"Andrew embodies the business philosophy described in Bob Burg and John David Mann's book 'The Go-Giver.' He is a young man wise beyond his years. I first met Andrew in a crowded room of business professionals, and was immediately impressed to learn he knew everyone by name. I later shared a business idea I was working on and he graciously set up a meeting to learn how he could help me brainstorm, problem solve and connect to people I needed to know. Andrew is a man of integrity -- and anyone in need of coaching or learning the skills needed to grow their network would benefit both professionally and personally by connecting with him!"

- **Lindy Chapman,** Consumer-focused Innovation in Real Estate & Relocation | RE Brokerage Owner | Startup Advisor | #LinkedinLive Beta Tester | Host, ReloTalk Podcast | Speaker

"Andrew is an enthusiastic and committed young man in pursuit of growth through his commitment to helping others. He has learned one of the most valuable life lessons. He fully understands he will find his greatest rewards and successes by helping others solve their problems and helping others succeed."

- **Peter Basica,** Founder of www.360smartercare.com & top-selling author of Post Covid-19 Communication & Leadership

"Andrew has been an incredible asset in helping me grow my business. He brings a fresh perspective and consistently offers practical, forward-thinking ideas that have made a meaningful impact on both my work and my life. More than that, Andrew is an extraordinary human being—he lives with heart-led purpose, yet moves with the clarity and focus of a business mind. His actions are thoughtful, intentional, and deeply rooted in compassion."

- **Janet Rosenbohm Child,** COPE Certified Health Coach & mother of 2

"Andrew Hall is a knowledgeable young man. He is passionate about his convictions and engaging when he explains his views. He knows how to break down complex concepts for participants to better understand the principles addressed. Andrew is definitely a great choice to train, teach and motivate an intergenerational audience."

- **Lori Beard,** CEO Steadfast Forward- Certified Life Coach for entrepreneurs ready to change their limiting thinking to live a life they love.

"Andrew is incredibly giving of his time and talent... He is wise beyond his years and a joy to work with."

- **Margo Duesterhaus,** President at Triple TeQ

"Andrew Hall is a genuine professional - he often puts others' needs above his own, and is always seeking a solution to problems. I've seen him work over the past couple of years and am always impressed with what he comes up with!"

- **Michael Volosen,** Human Resources Generalist

"Andrew is a great person that wants to help make a difference in the world. Thankful to have him as a friend and on my team of "advisors" when needed. Connect with Andrew and see how the two of you may be able to make the world a better place with your synergy."

- **SAM Morrison,** Helping businesses take their time back one task at a time, *Gratitude & Self-Love Expert | Founder, Safe Heart Connections*

"I had the pleasure of collaborating with Andrew for several years and got to witness first hand his many positive personal and professional characteristics. He is a strong leader of people, well attuned to business drivers, creative, tenacious, resilient, and passionate about customer service. He works well at either the strategic or tactical level and has a tremendous capacity to get things done and to connect you with powerful resources. I know Andrew can accomplish anything he wants to and will do it with a high degree of integrity. He is a great colleague, friend and person whom I recommend without hesitation."

- **Frank Mulcahy Sr.,** Behavioral Expert, International Cyber Security Advocate

"Andrew is an amazing executive coach for me. He makes sure I stay motivated and focused on my mission. His business and personal skills are exceptional and highly valued at OHVCC. He puts our mission first and helps me become the best leader I can be. Andrew is priceless in my life and I am honored to have him in my corner. I highly recommend Andrew to anyone looking to grow in their life and business."

- **Sheila Hensley,** CEO of OHVCC, and Founder of S3 for Veterans

"Andrew is one of the most honest and trustworthy persons I know. He works hard for his clients and truly appreciates referrals."

- the late, **Sandy Luedke,** BROKER / REALTOR® at Ideal Real Estate Group | Real Estate | Homes For Buying or Selling

"Andrew is trustworthy, quick witted, charismatic, and one of a kind. He is a natural born leader who inspires and gathers others effortlessly."

- **Garrison Gribbin,** Client Experience Associate at Fidelity Investments

"Andrew has a reputation for being a great connector and being very passionate about inspiring others to be the best they can be and growing their tribe! His mission is to connect you to people, resources and information that will all be valuable assets for your growth. His passion for inspiring and motivating others is very obvious when you first meet him. You will be glad that you chose Andrew Hall to be your partner in success as he is a true influencer and will make a difference in your business!!"

- **Steve Lester,** 35+ year Licensed Realtor at Fathom Realty

"Andrew is one of the go-getters of his generation! Great Christian, great connector, great friend. Wise beyond his years. Although he moved up north, he still has great connections in Texas and is always looking to connect me to someone. I wish I had known as much about my passions when I was his age!"

- **Coach Dale Young,** www.coachdale.com | Solid Foundations - Directed Results - Enduring Legacy

"Andrew has such a special way of inspiring the best within people! Not only has he been a massive connector and referral partner, he helped me to triple my prices for my services and own the value that I had to deliver to my clients. I've been able to sell more effectively and more congruently. Definitely connect with him to see how he can take your life, your business and your tribe to the next level!"

- **Christopher Burns,** Men's Life and Business Activation Coach

"I highly recommend Andrew! He is a business savvy connector of people and a valuable asset for anyone looking to grow."

- **Leslie Wilson,** Financial Services at Five Rings Financial, LLC

"I have known Andrew personally since May 2018 and am simply impressed by his level of dedication in being such a great friend. Just when I wasn't sure what direction I wanted to take with my career, Andrew pointed me in the right direction and helped me stay on track! Being connected to him has opened countless doors for me in the business world to connect with the best of the very best with those connections still friends of mine to this day! If you need help getting the right advice on moving your business forward or need help getting connected to the right people for your projects, Andrew is it and look no further!"

- **Elan Becker,** Founder, The Concierge Accountant

"Andrew Hall's heart, hustle, and wisdom ignite action in teens chasing big dreams. His 31 words, from "Quit" to "Humility," crush doubts with a mentor's push for purpose. His integrity and enthusiasm make him a trusted guide. This plan turns dreamers into doers, young or old. Grab it, young reader—Andrew's light leads to a life that shines!"

- **Ben Linville,** President, Webisoft USA

Life Coach Lori Beard's Foreword to *Coming of Age: 31 Words on How to be Wise Beyond Your Years by Andrew A. Hall*

My years of being a full-time mother of eight children ended when my youngest son started Kindergarten. At that time, I returned to school, earning certifications as a Life Coach and Clinical Hypnosis Practitioner.

Since marketing was a new concept for me, I heeded my mentor's advice to step out of my office to meet other professionals by attending networking events.

A couple of times into my new self-promoting adventure I noticed a witty and friendly young adult networking guru. This young man got my attention instantly. I would describe it as a "networking connection at first sight." Beyond helping me ease into this new practice due to his welcoming charisma, I also learned from his ability to master the art and science of networking. I noticed how this Congeniality-like being was and still is enthusiastic about strategically making succinct business connections. His recommendations are well thought out with the best interest in creating a cooperative opportunity that could potentially turn into mutually beneficial joint ventures.

These few interactions were enough to realize that Andrew Hall was wise beyond his years. Affectionately referred to as my 9th child, Andrew Hall is short in stature, nonetheless mighty in heart and mind. Why would I "adopt" a perfect stranger into the family? My eight children asked. The day to meet him arrived when he came over and enjoyed a Puerto Rican meal. He graciously complimented the chef, me. Both my children and my husband gave him the seal of approval.

One experience that was pivotal in our friendship happened when we both collaborated in a panel to discuss how to leverage millennials' unique talents despite generational differences in the business arena. The points presented by the panel impacted the audience positively.

An advocate for a harshly misunderstood generation, Andrew took this opportunity to highlight the ample contributions millennials have benefitted the world.

He was able to debunk fallacies explaining that engaging with millennials determines how successful a business will be. Some of his points that reinforced his statement include:

- Millennials value community, family, and creativity in their work;
- Millennials are not just virtually connected via social networks; they value the role that they play in these communities;
- Millennials are considered exceptional multitaskers, though brain science tells us that multitasking is a myth. More likely, they are clever at switching tasks quickly enough to appear to be doing them simultaneously;
- They prefer a collaborative work-culture rather than a competitive one;
- They are more tolerant of different races and groups than older generations.

This successful experience led me to invite him as a guest in my YouTube channel interview series. Once again, during the conversation, he exhibited high levels of entrepreneurial spirit combined with personal growth enthusiasm. He spoke about the books he's read and shared great quotes from memory, which was quite impressive.

The interview exchange must have hit him on a sweet spot because soon thereafter, Andrew approached me asking for help with one of his personal areas of struggle. I admired his desire to overcome this issue as it was incongruent with his moral and spiritual beliefs. He was determined to conquer it, which showed me his yearning to be spiritually aligned.

I felt fortunate to assist him by providing resources that empowered him in this honorable goal. This time, being wise beyond his years meant asking for help—another admirable attribute of Andrew. Recognizing his limitations led him to openly ask for help when he was feeling stuck, a manifestation of humility and sincerity in living a life of integrity.

One big accomplishment this refining process led him to was to take on the commitment of marrying the love of his life. I was able to witness the wedding reception in Texas. Watching him fulfill one of his biggest aspirations become a reality was a glorious and joyful experience for me. He is a devoted husband to his sweet Marissa and I have a feeling this dynamic duo will go places.

When he asked me to write this foreword, I felt honored as my heart pounded with joy! What a brilliant idea for a daily guide delivered as a morning devotional! Genius! This is another evidence of the wisdom beyond his years and now the world has access to some of it no matter the reader's age. Can we all benefit from more wisdom in our life? Yes, we can.

I guarantee you every page of *Coming of Age: How to Be Wise Beyond Your Years, a Guide and Devotional* is crammed full of useful hints and tips so that you can profit from them. I encourage you to do the work required by answering the carefully crafted questions designed to speed up your progress intended with the daily topics. Execution on the recommended action items will help you turn the theoretical information into valuable experiences for massive advancement. I agree with his aforementioned advice: "Embrace the feeling in this very moment of envisioning yourself completing this book. To complete is better than to begin."

Important note: As a student of success, I want to urge you to commit to the "further reading" recommendations Andrew offers. Each of these specially selected books will give you an opportunity to learn new things and explore new ideas to help you grow mentally, emotionally, and psychologically. They will increase your knowledge and make you smarter. Do I need to add, they will make you wise beyond your years? 😊

It has been my pleasure to know Andrew Hall since 2017 in a friendship that developed from business networking acquaintances into a mentoring partnership. An enthusiastic entrepreneur, a networking expert, intuitive connector, and personal development devotee striving for spiritual freedom, Andrew Hall is wise beyond his years. He is a great 'go-to' resource to help you navigate through your days in this journey called life with enlightened prudence.

Enjoy the self-evaluating and thought-provoking insights. Expect to gain a better understanding of yourself as I did when I read the forthcoming pages.

With much love and sincerity,

–Lori Beard

CEO, Steadfast Forward: Certified Life Coach for entrepreneurs ready to change their limiting thinking to live a life they love.

Email Lori at lori@steadfast-forward.com

Find Lori's book: *Freedom from Self-Slavery: The 7 Rs Method: A Guide for Self-Mastery and Empowerment*

Table of Contents:

Dedication vi

What the first reader had to say: viii

What others are saying about Andrew A. Hall x
and his strategies!

Life Coach Lori Beard's Foreword to xvi
*Coming of Age: 31 Words on How to be Wise Beyond
Your Years by Andrew A. Hall*

Preface - *A Call to Wisdom* 1

Day 1 - *The End* 3

Day 2 - *Service* 5

Day 3 - *Relationship* 7

Day 4 - *Quit* 9

Day 5 - *Listen* 11

Day 6 - *Try* 13

Day 7 - *Rest* 15

Day 8 - *Sowing* 17

Day 9 - *Labor* 19

Day 10 - *Foundation* 21

Day 11 - *Persistence* 23

Day 12 - *Peace* 25

Day 13 - *Margin* 27

Day 14 - *Clean* 29

Day 15 - *Consistent* 31

Day 16 - *Observation* 33

Day 17 - *Ambiguity* 35

Day 18 - *Save* 37

Day 19 - *Decision* 39

Day 20 - *Passion* 41

Day 21 - *Mirror* 43

Day 22 - *Forgive* 45

Day 23 - *Affirmation* 47

Day 24 - *Intentional* 49

Day 25 - *Children* 51

Day 26 - *Home* 53

Day 27 - *No Regrets* 55

Day 28 - *Patience* 57

Day 29 - *Guide* 59

Day 30 - *Fear* 61

Day 31 - *Humility* 63

Conclusion: 65

Resources: 67

Contact: 71

Keep in touch: 72

Acknowledgement: 73

About the author: 74

Preface
<u>A Call to Wisdom</u>

I sat in the sand, the sun dipping low, watching a boy of fourteen gaze beyond the waves. His eyes held questions—doubts, insecurities, dreams unshaped by experience. I saw myself in him, a young soul on the cusp of adulthood, yearning for answers. This book is for that boy, and for you, dear reader, stepping into life's vast sea.

Welcome, friend. Some call this a workbook, others a devotional. I call it a guide to rewrite your thoughts, to find wisdom. It's not a novel, not a trilogy—it's a 31-day path to grow wise beyond your years. Words shape our reality; wisdom knows which words, or silence, suit your unique journey. I wrote this for *you*, not others in your life. To maximize it, act. Take each chapter's word and apply it today. If you're not doing, this book may bore you. Wisdom lives in the experiment of living.

"We don't need more knowledge. We need wisdom to apply what we know." —Andrew A. Hall

Many seek wisdom as a byproduct of success, but wisdom is its foundation. She walks with you through sorrow and joy, elusive yet ever-present. I've caught her traces, like water in an open bowl while driving on a bumpy road, and poured them here. By this book's end, you'll recognize her in your choices, perhaps befriend her. Reread it, and Wisdom may reveal beauty only the wise see.

Make no mistake: you are an adult. I speak to you as one. Take action. Take wisdom. Immerse yourself in these pages and let them shape you. Are you thinking folly or seeking truth, lacking knowledge to form wise actions? This is your invitation to a journey of reflection and growth, to become not just wiser, but wise beyond your years.

Agur, son of Jakeh, said, "There are three things that are too amazing for me, four that I do not understand: the way of an eagle in the sky, the way of a snake on a rock, the way of a ship on the high seas, and the way of a man with a maiden" (Proverbs 30:18–19). You may never grasp Wisdom's dance fully, but this book starts your pursuit. She is the most precious of immaterial things. Wisdom is calling.

—Andrew A. Hall

Day 1
The End

You're lucky. You made it another day. How did you spend yesterday? Everything in wisdom begins with the knowledge of death, the end of your life. We are all destined to live once; *YOLO*. When a child is born, we triumphantly yell "what a glorious day it is," but ancient text states "better is the day of one's death than the day of one's birth." Why? Because it is the culmination of a life completed, a life well lived. Wisdom is knowing that completion is better than beginning. Death is the completion of life. *Embracing the knowledge of your end* gives you the proper perspective to live life more accurately every single day. Your days are numbered (even though you don't know the number). This book you've begun reading is full of thoughts that might be new to you. I encourage you to apply one of these *words* to your life and share it with a friend. Be careful–don't share it with a fool! And also, embrace the feeling, take a second, in this very moment. Envision yourself completing this book.

To state my point in a proverb: *To complete is better than to begin.*

Further Reading: The Obituary in your local paper and *Benjamin Franklin: An American Life* - Walter Isaacson

Coming of Age

Ponder: What would you like to accomplish before you complete your life? What's your dream?

_____

_____

_____

_____

_____

_____

_____

_____

_____

_____

_____

_____

_____

_____

_____

_____

_____

_____

Disclaimer: *Suicide is not the completion or wisdom this chapter describes. It's a tragic loss of life. If you're struggling, seek help from a trusted friend or professional (call 988 in the U.S.).*

Day 2
Service

Serving is a vice. Vice is defined as: a tool for holding. To be wise beyond your years, you'll discover that you're working for the things in life that will ultimately define you. If I say "Jesus," you might think of the savior of Christian believers. If I say "Hitler," you might think of an elected political leader who tried to take over the world while killing millions of innocent people. If I say "Bill Hemdrickle," and you say "who?" Exactly. You have no idea who Bill is, because that person never applied himself to a dedication of service to others on the scale that other famous influencers did. Bill didn't choose a vice of any kind. I'm sure he exists somewhere doing some infrequent good. But if you're going to be wise beyond your years, you'll want to make sure you are wrapped up in the vice of serving. Serving others produces influence and cultivates a tribe. It's a choice; it's _your_ choice. You can do whatever you'd like to do. Make a good choice to serve the greatest good like Jesus.

To state my point in a proverb: You choose the vice you are going to serve and you will serve it all your life.

Further Reading: _The Gospel according to John_ - The Apostle John

Coming of Age

Ponder: Which service will you be devoted to?

___

Day 3
Relationship

Imagine a big boat. There you are at the helm: the captain. Smell the salt water and the sunrise melting the sleep from your face. Relationship is just that: a ship. You use this ship to relate to others. If you have a "friendship" then you're relating as friends. There's a little known fact that atoms (which are what all matter is made up of) do not have an actual connection point. They never "touch"; they actually have constant space between each atom that makes up a substance. You could say that each atom has a *relationship* with another atom. Every object or being you encounter in your life offers an opportunity to relate. You're obligated to engage with each one. How you choose to sail these relationships determines your success in life. If you abuse human relationships, you will find that human relationships will have nothing of substance to offer you in the future. If you abuse your relationship with your car, you will find your car breaking down more frequently. *Everything* in life is a relationship. If you are choosing to be wise beyond your years, you will leverage everything that comes into your life for the highest and best outcome.

To state my point in a proverb: Everything is relational.

Further Reading: *How to Win Friends and Influence People* - Dale Carnegie

Coming of Age

Ponder: What or whom are you relating? How can you improve that relationship right now?

_____

_____

_____

_____

_____

_____

_____

_____

_____

_____

_____

_____

_____

_____

_____

_____

Day 4
Quit

Notice that I didn't say "quitter."

To quit is very different from being a "quitter." Throughout life, you will struggle and wrestle with the thoughts of quitting something. I encourage you to quit. Quit smoking. Quit pornography. Quit unhealthy eating. Quit drunkenness. Quit illegal behavior. Quit bad habits. Quit hanging with bad friends. Quit laziness. Wisdom is discovering the paths that lay before you and deciding which one will get you to your desired outcome. Quitting something is often that very path. But therein lies the decision (to cut away from) of *what to quit*. In the "success training world," you'll hear things like "quitters never win and winners never quit" ... this teaching is not from an enlightened speaker. They must be speaking to perfect people with perfect habits, in which case, to quit anything would be a negative step. But, if you're going to be wise beyond your years, you need to quit things and quit them *fast*! Don't waste a minute of your life on something you'll regret. The nursing homes of the elderly are filled with regret. Say it with me: "*I quit.*"

To state my point in a proverb: Quitting is the first step to beginning something new.

Further Reading: *How to Say No to a Stubborn Habit–even if you feel like saying Yes* - Erwin W. Lutzer

Coming of Age

Ponder: What will you quit today?

_____
_____
_____
_____
_____
_____
_____
_____
_____
_____
_____
_____
_____
_____
_____
_____
_____
_____

Day 5
Listen

Listening is not an activity done just with your ears. Listening is an all-encompassing, fully engrossed, experience. The heart, ears, and your soul.

When anyone speaks, they intend to be heard, to be listened to. Listening does come through our ears but it also comes through our emotions, our skin, our cells, the compost of who we are and how God has made us. Our experiences are our lens: it's how we hear.

Do you actually put yourself in the shoes and shirt of the person speaking? Have you ever been trying to get your parents attention and they say "go on Beth, wait, what were you saying?" or "I can hear you now Roy, say it one more time." To be wise beyond your years is to mature enough to understand you shouldn't brush off people trying to speak to you, and you shouldn't stop your important activity to give your attention to someone undeserving. In your conversations, you can do the opposite of this by taking care of your own insecurities first. By reading this book you're investing in your growth. This allows you to be fully engaged in your friend's words. I have a friend, named Caleb, who is one of the world's best listeners. He asks a question and waits like a golden retriever just anticipating your answer! The world stops as he waits to listen to your valuable reply. How does he do that? He cares. Your words *matter* to him. Be that kind of a listener! Listen with everything you have got within you. Let the other person know that you care deeply. This will serve your relationships for many years to come.

To state my point in a proverb: Listening should end with a list of what the other person said.

Further Reading: *Crucial Conversations Tools for Talking When Stakes Are High, Second Edition* – Kerry Patterson, Joseph Grenny, Ron McMillan, and Al Switzler

Coming of Age

Ponder: Who do you know who is an amazing listener? Describe them here:

Day 6
Try

"To do, or not to do, there is no try" –Yoda. What a dumb statement! Sure, you can see the value in having faith and not doubting. To try with faith is approved. To try while doubting is to not try at all. I implore you to try. Try something you've never done before; try to give, taste, smell, bid, trade, sell, grow or do something that is completely novel to you. Trying, in essence, is wisdom. For wisdom is applied knowledge and knowledge is never certain, it is approximate or near certain at best. Therefore, to apply knowledge, which is not 100 percent guaranteed accurate, is to "try." Try something new today, and make it a habit to try something, learn something, or do something you've never done. Trying is part of the process of growth. Now, I tell you this wisdom within the context of knowing good from evil. Don't try the vices that have killed greatness within mankind throughout history. Don't try stupid things that you don't believe will succeed. Don't try something you care absolutely nothing about. But rather do try something new to you.

Go on, try it.

To state my point in a proverb: Try, fail, adjust, try again, fail again, succeed

Further Reading: _Psycho-Cybernetics_ - Dr. Maxwell Maltz

Coming of Age

Ponder: What will you try today?

_____

_____

_____

_____

_____

_____

_____

_____

_____

_____

_____

_____

_____

_____

_____

_____

_____

_____

Day 7
Rest

Sleep. Sabbath. Rest. The reason you're reading this book is because you are very much, in your particular arena, an ambitious person. You desire wisdom to be made manifest in your life. Resting is a non-negotiable in life. Your body will eventually not perform at its optimal level if you don't rest. Now, let me say, there are various levels of resting. The first one is sleep. You must protect your sleep! Narcotics, stimuli, etc., just won't serve you in the long term. Your body was designed to heal itself. You might need six hours per night, you might need nine hours. Personally, I require about nine hours of sleep every night. Some of my workaholic friends (I have many) would believe that I'm wasting 3-5 hours/day of productivity. I am not. I'm rejuvenating my body, my mind, my spirit, and my relationship with myself. Sleep is critical for my life's goals. Another aspect of rest is a weekly day off. In almost every language there is a day called "the day of rest." Find that day for you and require nothing of yourself. Treat it like "fun money" you can do anything you want to relax and rejuvenate. On my sabbath day I sleep in, take a bath, walk, think, watch some interesting spiritual content, and maybe do some project that's strictly personal. There's something special, or even divine, about a 7-day week. Lastly, I'd recommend finding an annual or bi-annual rest. Most folks call it a "vacation." I like to think of it as a multi-day strategy session to plan my next six months. Why try to become wise beyond your years if you never choose to rest?

To state my point in a proverb: The soul must rest

Further Reading: *The Power of Rest* - Gary Keesee

Coming of Age

Ponder: How did you accomplish rest today?

Day 8
Sowing

As long as the earth remains, there will always be seedtime and harvest time (a time to reap the profit of what you have sown). If you look around the entire world, there is a spring season, there is a summer season, there is a fall season and there is a winter season. Most people fantasize about life full of *summertime* and *springtime* but that is not wisdom. Wisdom is embracing each season as it is. You are human. You do not dictate the seasons. You can only dictate what you *do* in each of those seasons. During winter you prepare the soil. Sowing into the soil is what you do in spring and summer, and in the harvest season, you harvest. That's what you do. If there is no *sowing*, then there is no *harvest*. If you want to be wise beyond your years, sow during the sowing seasons and harvest during the harvest seasons. I encourage you to have a preset system that allows you to identify the differences between sowing seasons and harvest seasons for your life.

"You must get good at one of two things: planting in the spring or begging in the fall" –Jim Rohn

To state my point in a proverb: Hear the lifesong and dance to the rhythm of each of the seasons of life.

Further Reading: *The Go-Giver* - Bob Burg & John David Mann

Coming of Age

Ponder: What did you sow today?

Day 9
Labor

Step one: Choose satisfying work.

Step two: Be satisfied in your work.

Labor is not your job (although it can be). You choose to find a labor of love (or hate). It is completely up to you to choose to labor at something that you love to do, whatever that may be. A wise person will seek out a labor which they can carry out to its end. You'll want to love the activities, regardless of getting paid, and yet–get paid abundantly for your labor. Many fools see labor as the enemy. "The impediment to action advances action. What stands in the way becomes the way." - Marcus Aurelius, philosopher and emperor. In order to show yourself truly wise beyond your years, you must develop a lifestyle that you love. Labor in life is inevitable. Many fools avoid labor and think they have won the "game of life." That fool has *lost* the game of life. YOU choose your life's contribution, your reward, and the legacy. Begin by choosing something you love. "Most people become rich by doing what they love. Almost no one accumulates wealth by working a job they hate." -Garrett Gunderson, chief wealth architect at Wealth Factory.

To state my point in a proverb: Labor births the joy of life.

Further Reading: *Do What You Love, the Money Will Follow* - Marsha Sinetar

Coming of Age

Ponder: Did you love your labor today?

Day 10
Foundation

Without a solid foundation, nothing good or evil can be built. You may wonder, "Why is this thing I'm doing not succeeding?" It is a result of having no solid foundation on which to build it. Building a business faster won't make it last longer. Building it slower won't make it last longer. Dating longer won't make your marriage more successful. It is solely based on the foundation on which it is built. No empire can succeed without a foundation. What foundation do you want to build for your life? What foundation have you already built? Many adults wish that they had the ability to go back and recreate the foundation of their life. Today you are laying the foundation for tomorrow just like today you're standing on the foundation of what you built yesterday. Today you're building your reputation, your knowledge, your experience, etc. Always remember there is "a time to break down, and a time to build up" –King Solomon of Israel. Evaluate your current foundation. Being wise beyond your years requires laying the foundation for your success intentionally.

To state my point in a proverb: Today is the last day of your past and the first day of the rest of your life, live well.

Further Reading: *The Book of Proverbs* - Solomon and others

Coming of Age

Ponder: Ask someone, "What would you change about your childhood foundation if you were given the chance?" Write *your* answer here.

_____

_____

_____

_____

_____

_____

_____

_____

_____

_____

_____

_____

_____

_____

_____

_____

Day 11
Persistence

This is the taproot of success. There is a small difference between consistent and persistent. You want to be both, but I believe persistence has another added ingredient in it. To be consistent is what everyone already is–taking a shower consistently, brushing your teeth consistently, sleeping consistently, going to work or school consistently–it's really nothing more than a habit. Consistent is a great place to start, but to become wise beyond your years you need to step into persistence. Persistence is to continue being consistent regardless of the circumstances. It's very close to focusing on one course until successful. If you're not focused on one thing, it's quite difficult to persist. If it becomes difficult to do the accurate thing, do it anyway. There's so much wisdom found in doing things that are difficult. Not for the sake of doing difficult things, but rather to make you become greater than your circumstances. You persist until you win, whatever it takes. If being consistent was all it took to be successful, more people would do it, but to be persistent is to do as Winston Churchill once proclaimed: "Success is going from failure to failure without the loss of enthusiasm." That is persistence and that mindset will serve you for a lifetime. Persist on that one thing with such passion and enthusiasm that I'll buy a ticket to your performance at Carnegie Hall, or fly in your spaceship to Mars, or vote for you in an election.

To state my point in a proverb: Perspire to inspire your aspirations to completion.

Further Reading - *Think and Grow Rich* - Napoleon Hill

Ponder: Identify one area of your life that you wish you had persisted in.

_____
_____
_____
_____
_____
_____

Make the decision to never feel that way again.

_____
_____
_____
_____
_____
_____
_____

Day 12
Peace

You've been in close proximity to these specific people. You've seen it in their eyes: no fear. It's not because they aren't afraid of something in their life, they simply have an attitude within them. They have a perspective that enables them to have peace in their mind and a "knowingness" in their heart that, as I'm sure you've heard them say, "Everything is going to be okay." Where does this peace come from? Most of the people I have asked, tell me it's their faith. Faith, defined by an ancient text is "the substance of things hoped for, the evidence of things not yet seen." So if they say it's their faith, how do I get that in my life? Faith is a muscle. It begins with the small things. When you don't hear from a loved one do you start to have fear, or do you believe that "everything will be okay"?

    Start here this week: When you're not sure what to do, let the peace come from your _faith_ that everything is going to be okay. It's a sign of maturity to not worry about things you can't control. "It makes no sense to worry about things you have no control over because there's nothing you can do about them, and why worry about things you don't control?" –Wayne Dyer, Successful Life Coach. Peace to you my friend!

To state my point in a proverb: A piece of peace is not peace; be whole.

Further Reading: _Life Without Limits: Inspiration for a Ridiculously Good Life_ - Nick Vujicic

Coming of Age

Ponder: How did you implement your faith today?

_____
_____
_____
_____
_____
_____
_____
_____
_____
_____
_____
_____
_____
_____
_____
_____

Day 13
Margin

Breathe in... breathe out. You just created *margin* in your life. Your days are numbered. In plain English, that means you're going to die someday. Someday in the future, your life will end and people left here on earth will say words about you. Maybe they'll even write books about you. Keanu Reeves was once asked, "What happens when we die?" He replied, "I know that the ones who love us will miss us." Margin is taking the time we have now to meditate on the things and people which matter most to us. The *who*, the *what*, the *why*, or even the *how* of what our lives are composed of needs attention during this life. If you have no margin and you're simply hustling from one task to another, then you'll wake up one day and wonder, "What happened to my life?" Take your time. Protect your time. Time is a finite resource. Give to yourself the blessing of an unplanned morning in the middle of the week with no obligations: just you, a pen, paper, and silence. Margin allows you to become wise beyond your years.

To state my point in a proverb: A profitable life is found in the margin.

Further Reading: *With: Reimagining the way you relate to God -* Skye Jethani

Ponder: How did you create *margin* in your life today?

Day 14
Clean

Clean was my word-of-the-year in 2018. It was powerful. Your wisdom must be found clean. Let me explain what I mean. Dirty is the antithesis of clean. Are your thoughts dirty? Is your heart dirty? Are your dishes dirty? Ancient text says "Where there are no oxen, the stable is clean." This is true in the symbolism that things which don't work, produce no dirt. If you look at all life here on earth, it came from dirt. You are, by nature (pun intended), dirty. However, you're not meant to stay that way. You're meant to be clean, and this requires work. You must work to clean the stable where the oxen have made it dirty. Remember that in order to be wise beyond your years, you must purify yourself—your mind, your thoughts, your motives. Clean is an action word. You say you want to make the world a better place. I don't believe you. Not unless, you are cleaning what is around you, what is within your power to clean. Purity is a similar word that could go here, but clean is better. Clean your room. Clean your life. Clean what is yours.

To state my point in a proverb: Be active and be clean.

Further Reading: *Freedom from Self-Slavery: The 7 Rs Method: A Guide for Self-Mastery and Empowerment* - Lori Beard

Coming of Age

Ponder: What did you clean today?

Day 15
Consistent

Drip, drip, drip, drip, drip, drip, drip... consistency is the mother of all skill. Some would say repetition. They're very close to each other in nature. I like consistency better than just reps. You can do one hundred thousand steps today or ten thousand steps every day for ten days. You're going to produce _vastly_ different results. Consistency should be tied directly to your daily agenda. If you're not doing something daily, you're not doing it consistently, in my opinion. You eat everyday, that's consistency. You miss lunch once a month, and it's not going to matter because you're mostly consistent. Your default setting is to eat lunch. What if you're consistently reading books on success or religion? You'd become more knowledgeable on those topics. Consistency is greater than intensity. Since you're a person who wants to be wise beyond your years, I implore you to use consistency in your finances, your relationships, your purpose. Consider your ways. Now, here's the "life hack" you've been looking for, one that will help you get started being consistent.

Make it:
1. Easy to do
2. Something you enjoy, both the process and inevitable result.

That's it! That's the key. Are you going to enjoy having 6-12 months of cash set aside for investing in the accurate opportunity? Then start in middle school to set aside an easy percentage of your income. Are you going to enjoy doing 100 sit-ups? NO! But can you do one? One will make you feel good. Then next week you can do two. Then the next week after that, you can do three or four. Consistency over intensity. In a year, you'll be able to do 100 and your body will look amazing for the rest of your life! Keep it simple: easy, and enjoy both the process & result. Start today.

To state my point in a proverb: When you do it again, it then becomes a gain.

Further Reading: _Slight Edge_ - Jeff Olson

Coming of Age

Ponder: Define what you desire to become consistent at:

Day 16
Observation

Observe the world around you. There's so much here if we just open our eyes. Understand this truth: You exist in a world that was here before you, and you can change it by interacting with it. In order to make a difference in something, you have to make an observation of what is. Start with what is in front of you. Is it a person? What are they feeling? Emotions. Why are they feeling those emotions? All these questions will help you come to the accurate understanding of what you can do to make the world a better place.

Make sure you:

1. Go deep enough in your observation. Don't just say to yourself, "That person is sad. How unfortunate." Ask yourself "why" five times when you're observing something. This will change your life.
2. Widen the view in your observation. Don't say to yourself, "A man hurt me, therefore all men are bad guys." Acknowledge that the specific man who hurt you might be evil, but also go wide enough in your observations to understand *many* other men are good men who won't hurt you.

Observation has to be both deep and wide in order to be wise beyond your years. This goes into your spiritual life, your emotional life, your relational life, and even your relationship with yourself. You can be wise beyond your years if you make an observation before making a decision. All of science begins with observation. Quality service begins with observation. A new relationship begins with observation.

To state my point in a proverb: Observe, behold, and influence. You cannot intentionally influence what you don't observe.

Further Reading: *Man's Search for Meaning* - Victor Frankl

Coming of Age

Ponder: What did you observe today that you didn't observe before?

_____
_____
_____
_____
_____
_____
_____
_____
_____
_____
_____
_____
_____
_____
_____
_____
_____
_____
_____
_____

Day 17
Ambiguity

Don't be so certain. Certainty is the identical twin of arrogance. You must always leave a small percentage of room for error, chance and interpretation. *The scientific method* uses this philosophy. They take a thought, an idea, or a hypothesis and do massive amounts of testing to make it into a theory. Once a theory, you can do many more tests for many years with many people, then you can call it a law. Even laws can be superseded by other laws. So in your life, develop some hypotheses. Find other wise people's laws and theories. Find what works really well for you and your life. Begin in the present moment of your life. Then hold these thoughts loosely, because at any time you could find a different law that supersedes your current laws. Always, my friend, leave a little room for ambiguity and what you don't fully know. I am certain of my uncertainty.

To state my point in a proverb: Certainty is a sister to arrogance and the father of humiliation.

Further Reading: *Things I wish I'd known before I got married* - Gary Chapman

Coming of Age

Ponder: Which hypothesis did you test today?

Day 18
Save

Saving is a shield. Saving is something your future self will thank you for. But saving is so much more than money. Saving your words. Saving your equity. Saving your relationships. Saving your dreams. Save could also mean *rescue*. Synonyms offer clarity to commonly used words. To *rescue* your money, you're saving yourself from future regret and pain. This is a habit that can save you in other ways. Money, as an example, provides a tangible component to immaterial value which makes it an easy scale to measure *saving*. If you begin saving in your youth, you can then use that money later as a safety net. If you want to be wise beyond your years, then treat your money as if you were old. Old people know that recession, depression, inflation, insurance, taxes, and crashes are all going to happen. Make your own personal decision to never have less than six months of your expenses set aside in an interest-bearing savings account with instant access. This will prove you're wise beyond your years. "Industry and frugality are the means of procuring wealth and thereby securing virtue." - Benjamin Franklin, co-founder of the United States of America.

To state my point in a proverb: Lack in life is solely a lack of saving.

Further Reading: *The Richest Man in Babylon* - George S. Clason

Coming of Age

Ponder: What do you have saved?

___

What would you like to have rescued?

___

Day 19
Decision

An incision means to cut into. A *decision* means to cut away from. Ancient texts often tell stories of fortune and misfortune; unfortunately you don't always know the truth hidden inside. I hope that you pursue wisdom and gather up this word: Decide. Every "yes" you say to one thing, you're saying "no" to a thousand other things. To decide means to cut away from. Cutting a piece of paper with scissors is painful for the paper. Emotionally, when you walk away from a relationship you "break up," cutting away from it. When you engage in a relationship like marriage, you marry one person and "cut away from" all other potential mates. Every time you decide anything, you are cutting out other things. So be wise beyond your years – cut away from the things that are bad for you, or not the *best for* you. Jody Victor, decamillionaire businessman, has said many times "*Go where you're celebrated, not tolerated.*" Decide today to be successful, and therefore cut away from habits that hinder your success. Decide to be honorable and cut away from anything dishonorable. Decide to cut away from pride and instead, practice humility. Decide once and for all that you will be wise, and therefore cut away from all foolishness.

Decide right now.

To state my point in a proverb: Decide boldly, for each cut crafts the masterpiece of you.

Further Reading: *The Choice: A Surprising New Message of Hope* - Og Mandino (one of Jody Victor's favorite authors)

Coming of Age

Ponder: In which specific area of your life is indecision hindering your success?

Day 20
Passion

Pati is the latin root word for passion, it means to *suffer*. Yes, *suffer*. When you find something you're passionate about, you'll continue doing it, regardless of the suffering involved in that task. This is why people say, "Find what you're passionate about and do that!" It's an objectively true statement. If you're not willing to suffer for what you are doing, STOP! Keep reading this book and find the wisdom of what you are passionate about. What's your niche? What sparks joy in your heart when you indulge in its execution? I only write to world changers – if you're reading this, you have greatness within you. There is something you are passionate about! If you're not passionate about anything yet, begin with curiosity. What are you curious about? You'll find your passion and suffer with joy.

To state my point in a proverb: Suffer for only that which you consciously intend to suffer for and nothing else.

Further Reading: *The Renaissance Soul: How to Make Your Passions Your Life—A Creative and Practical Guide* - Margaret Lobenstine

Coming of Age

Ponder: What do you take joy in suffering in?

Day 21
Mirror

Mirrors are common in first-world nations, yet there's something truly unique and spectacular about seeing yourself in one. An ancient text says, "A man looks at a mirror, but when he leaves, he forgets what he has seen." When you gaze into a mirror, you see the texture of yourself—your face, your skin tone, your hair. But if you look into the eyes staring back at you, you can peer into your own soul. Not *what*, but *who* do you see? To be wise beyond your years is to look into the mirror and love yourself for who you are today. You're not perfect, and you never will be. As a child, you dreamed of your teenage self; at sixteen, you imagined your twenties. When you're on your death bed late in life, you'll realize that all your past selves hoped you'd reach your full potential. To live with true wisdom is to embrace the person in the mirror and sow the seeds of greatness into your heart. Your future self will thank you eye-to-eye.

A proverb to live by: The mirror show's a person worthy of some contemplation.

For more on mirrors, read *The Magic of Believing* by Claude Bristol, especially the chapter "The Mirror Technique."

Coming of Age

Ponder: What do you want to see in the mirror in 3–5 years?

Day 22
Forgive

It may seem obvious. Forgiveness allows you to "move on." But it's a little deeper than you may expect. Ask yourself this question: Have I forgiven myself? Think about it. That thing you did that hurt someone else. After you've asked them for forgiveness, did you forgive yourself? The enemy of mankind doesn't want you to forgive yourself. You are not immune from self-deprecation. Forgive yourself.

Wisdom is to forgive ALL: Others that are under your authority; others that are not under your authority; decisions you made that failed; decisions you made that are a success; God; your father; your mother; yourself.

What! Forgive God?! (If you serve God, you probably believe in a perfect being–incapable of doing wrong). Yes! Although He has done *nothing* wrong against you, you have not forgiven Him of your *perceived* offense. The first man declared with gravitas authority "the woman You gave me..." caused this sin to happen. Stop blaming God. Forgive him of the *perceived* offense.

Forgive ALL.

Also, if you are harboring bitterness and unforgiveness, it is a poison that kills you, and does nothing to the offender. Forgive ALL.

To state my point in a proverb: In order to forgive, you must go first and fore-give.

Further study: *A Beautiful Day in the Neighborhood* - movie about Mister Rogers

Coming of Age

Ponder: Who do you need to forgive today? What for?

Day 23
<u>Affirmation</u>

Affirm: "to offer emotional support or encourage" continually, continually, continually, and on and on... I encourage you to "make your dreams come true." I love this statement because so few understand it. Let me explain: In order to "make your dreams come true" you have to admit that in their current form, they are a lie. Dreams begin as lies. This is not what you've been told before. In order for your lies to become true, you have to write them down, create a plan of action, then implement that plan of action consistently. You are then, with your words and actions, "affirming" your dreams, and telling them that they will "come true." So remember deep inside of you that you can make a dream into a reality by affirming it beyond mere words and more than misguided actions. It's a combination of thoughts, words, and actions that create a reality that you can step into and live.

To state my point in a proverb: Be firm in your imagination.

Further Reading: *Hung by the Tongue* - Francis P. Martin

Coming of Age

Ponder: What dreams are you affirming right now?

Day 24
Intentional

Wisdom is not haphazard. It is a learned process. It is applied knowledge. As you're asking questions in life you may have the thought cross your mind: "Why are some people more wise than others?" That is solely because of intentionality. Intention, at a very simple level, is your desire in a focused manner. You might have the desire to become an author. If you stop there, it'll just be a wish. But if you turn that desire into the intention of, "I'm going to write a book." Then you've used intention to make yourself an author. Thus, accomplishing your desire. How does one live intentionally? Well, it's quite simple, it's coming up with the desire and making it clear. Once it's clear, you can put your energy behind that clarity–that is the formula for being intentional.

One last thought: Don't just possess intentionality, BE intentional. Be an intentional person in everything that is within your grasp to be intentional about... and leave a little room for spontaneity.

To state my point in a proverb: Intend, contend, and ascend

Further Reading: *Intentional Living* - John C. Maxwell

What result has been eluding you and how can you be intentional about procuring it?

Day 25
Children

"Be innocent as a child." You may have heard this phrase. I'm not sure that it's accurate. I would say, and wisdom supports, that you should be as *real* as children. When a child lies, you know it. When a child laughs, even the most sinister among us, laughs with them.

Children is a word of wisdom because studying children is the best place to gather insight to become truly honest and authentic. This concept is the root of the phrase "be innocent as a child." Children are not innocent, but rather authentic. Study children, how they are joyous and sincere. For in doing this, you see a mirror of yourself. Also note, that "authentic" and "innocent" doesn't mean skip imitation. We are to imitate good deeds and good thoughts but impersonating forever draws us away from who we truly are in our deepest levels. Be authentic. Be yourself.

To state my point in a proverb: Wisdom from the mouth of babes, no... wisdom from the hearts of authentic children.

Further Reading: *Integrity: The Courage to Meet the Demands of Reality* - Dr. Henry Cloud

Coming of Age

Ponder: Are you being true? Yes / no

Day 26
Home

This word strikes a chord in all of us. You maybe had a bad home growing up. You might have been beyond blessed with a "good home." Sadly, home is a place that most people never truly experience. They go from place to place, thing to thing, job to job, spouse to spouse, and never truly feel at home. This is a tragedy because home is not a place...it is an experience. I implore you, make wherever you are today "_home_." Make whomever you're with your home. Redefine home as the place you serve others and give wisdom to those around you. I feel most at home when I'm experiencing this quote by Timothy Keller. "To be loved but not known is comforting but superficial. To be known and not loved is our greatest fear. But to be fully known and truly loved is, well, a lot like being loved by God. It is what we need more than anything. It liberates us from pretense, humbles us out of our self-righteousness, and fortifies us for any difficulty life can throw at us."

To state my point in a proverb: Don't find home, make a home.

Further Reading: _The 360 Degree Leader: Developing Your Influence from Anywhere in the Organization_ - John Maxwell

Coming of Age

Ponder: What did you do today to make your home?

_____
_____
_____
_____
_____
_____
_____
_____
_____
_____
_____
_____
_____
_____
_____
_____

Day 27
No Regrets

Success speaker and author Stephen Covey Sr. once wrote "begin with the end in mind." What's your end? Have you asked someone near the end of their life any deep questions? You'll be amazed at what you might find. As a child, you believed you needed to please those around you. As you got older you realized that people aren't thinking about you, but rather themselves. When you're young, you think about making mistakes and how they could seem irreversible. As you get older you realize it's the things you never tried that slowly erode you the most–regret. "I wish I would have tried..." Part of my "no regrets" mindset is writing this book. I've been told countless times that I'm "wise beyond my years." Well, what if I never write my thoughts down for others to receive that same compliment and create a future for themselves? Then I'd live with regret. I can't live with that regret when I'm older. I'm going to do the best I can right now. I'm going to invest my time into you...because I love you. I love your passion and drive to become wise. Keep learning, keep studying, keep trying. You're going to get there! Review what Gary Keller wrote in one of the last chapters of *The ONE Thing*. The top 5 things those near death regret: it's what they didn't do.

To state my point in a proverb: Regret not, for it is an undying horror.

Further Reading: *The ONE Thing, the surprisingly simple truth behind extraordinary results* - Gary Keller

Coming of Age

What will you not regret?

Day 28
Patience

When you're wise beyond your years, you understand that time is a tool that can be used in your favor. I love to hear my wife say "Your future-self thanks you!" Patience is not inaction, although it may seem that way. "Patience is a virtue" as the saying goes. Sadly, most interpret this to mean "doing nothing is actually good."

Wrong.

Patience, rather, is the action of time. Instead of putting money into a problem to fix it, you put time into it. This does not mean *effort*, it means *time*.

"Time heals all" is another false paradigm so don't go too far to the other side of the road into the other "ditch." Don't believe that time without action is going to solve a problem you're avoiding. Just apply patience today. Apply time to an issue to let time work on your problem for you.

To state my point in a proverb: Patience is truly the ultimate passive action.

Further Reading: *The Compound Effect* - Darren Hardy

Coming of Age

Wonder: How have you confused inaction with patience?

Day 29
Guide

Don't be the hero or the person with all the answers. Be the guide to help others come to their own decisions on their own. You are no one's hero, you are the guide. The philosophy that you need to be #1 in your chosen field is obviously self-serving. Try the alternative. Be the guide. In every great story, there is a hero. For certain seasons of your life, you must be the hero. But another character that turns great movies into cinematography legends, is the *guide*. In your quest to seek wisdom, seek a guide. And more importantly, BE a guide. Find someone who is a little behind you. Charles Dickens once said "No one is useless in this world who lightens the burden of another." Guides do this. Go, and lighten the burden of another today. That person you know who is just a grade or a step behind you—mentor them, guide them. Be the guide, that's the real hero.

To state my point in a proverb: Be a hero to the hero.

Further Reading: *Building a Story Brand* - Donald Miller

Coming of Age

Ponder: Who is someone you can help guide today?

Day 30
Fear

You've probably heard it before: "The fear of the Lord is the beginning of wisdom."

That's straight from ancient scripture. And if you don't believe me, look it up yourself. Now, when we hear "fear," we usually think of being scared. But in this case, it's deeper than that. "To fear or to have reverence and extreme humility before someone or something that is so much greater or worthy than you,"—that is the beginning of wisdom. It's about reverence. It's knowing your place in the presence of something far greater—and responding with humility. That's where wisdom starts, but it's not where it ends. When you feel fear, remember it's an emotion predicated on internal or external circumstances. When fear comes across your mind, ask yourself, "Is this fear worthy of my heart?" From that answer you can decide how much of your thoughts you let "fear" consume.

Running from a wild bear in the woods... should consume all of your thoughts.

Wondering what other people think of you... should consume very little of your thoughts.

To state my point in a proverb: Fear never understanding fear.

Further Reading: *Wild at Heart* - John Eldridge

Coming of Age

Ponder: How has reverent fear hindered or helped your success?

Day 31
Humility

I can talk for a whole hour on this one word. Humility is powerful and sadly it's often misunderstood. Pride is the antithesis of humility. Pride is very rampant in our culture, and I can swear to you, pride has always been rampant in every culture. Therefore, to be humble makes you distinct. Different. Wise.

    I have to caution you, although humiliation's root word is humble, *humiliation* is a terrible word that has NOTHING to do with being humble. Humiliation is what your parents may have subconsciously taught you to believe was being humble. Humble, rather, is the intentional placement of yourself below those around you. Humble is being the strongest in the room, and serving everyone. If you were raised with "humble means", then you think being humble is *lacking* something. But being humble is having everything you can in abundance and still choosing to lower yourself beneath your principles, your moral code, your God, your study, your authority, etc. Seeking humility is the pursuit of a lifetime, but it is the best use of your life. Invest some time in the area in which you excel, by finding one or more ways to humble yourself. Pick up trash that isn't yours. Stand up for a stranger. Be honest to the authority when everyone else is lying. Try it. It's the hardest thing you'll ever do.

Life hack: Fasting is an ancient path to humility—simple, powerful, and forgotten by most.

To state my point in a proverb: Humble yourself in life, or be humiliated by life.

Further Reading: *Humility, Updated Edition* - Andrew Murray

Ponder: Will you choose to practice humility? Yes / no

How so?

Conclusion:

There is no conclusion to wisdom. There is only application of wisdom - the key is not the words, the key is *LIVING* the Words.

Keep learning, understanding and applying.

Your guide in Wisdom,

Resources:

Day 1, The end: *Your local obituary & Benjamin Franklin: An American Life* - Walter Isaacson

Day 2, Service: *The Gospel according to John*

Day 3, Relationship: *How to Win Friends and Influence People* - Dale Carnegie

Day 4, Quit: *How to Say No to a Stubborn Habit–even if you feel like saying Yes* - Erwin W. Lutzer

Day 5, Listen: *Crucial Conversations Tools for Talking When Stakes Are High, Second Edition* – Kerry Patterson, Joseph Grenny, Ron McMillan, and Al Switzler

Day 6, Try: *Psycho-Cybernetics* - Dr. Maxwell Maltz

Day 7, Rest: *The Power of Rest* - Gary Keesee

Day 8, Sowing: *The Go-Giver* - Bob Burg & John David Mann

Day 9, Labor: *The Richest Man in Babylon* - George S. Clason

Day 10, Foundation: *The Book of Proverbs* - Solomon and others

Day 11, Persistence: *Think and Grow Rich* - Napoleon Hill

Day 12, Peace: *Life Without Limits: Inspiration for a Ridiculously Good Life* - Nick Vujicic

Day 13, Margin: *Do What you Love, The Money Will Follow* - Marsha Sinetar

Day 14, Clean: *Freedom from Self-Slavery: The 7 Rs Method: A Guide for Self-Mastery and Empowerment* - Lori Beard

Day 15, Consistent: *The Slight Edge: Turning Simple Disciplines into Massive Success and Happiness* – Jeff Olson

Day 16, Observation: *Man's Search for Meaning* - Viktor Frankl

Day 17, Ambiguity: *Things I wish I'd known before I got married* - Gary Chapman

Day 18, Save: *The Richest Man in Babylon* - George S. Clason

Day 19, Decision: *The Choice: A Surprising New Message of Hope* - Og Mandino

Day 20, Passion: *The Renaissance Soul: How to Make Your Passions Your Life—A Creative and Practical Guide* - Margaret Lobenstine

Day 21. Mirror: "The Mirror Technique." *The Magic of Believing* - Claude Bristol

Day 22, Forgive: *A Beautiful Day in the Neighborhood*

Day 23, Affirmation: *Hung by the Tongue* - Francis P. Martin

Day 24, Intentional: *Intentional Living: Choosing a Life That Matters* - John C. Maxwell

Day 25, Children: *Integrity: The Courage to Meet the Demands of Reality* - Dr. Henry Cloud

Day 26, Home: *The 360 Degree Leader: Developing Your Influence from Anywhere in the Organization* - John Maxwell

Day 27, No Regrets: *The ONE Thing, the surprisingly simple truth behind extraordinary results* - Gary Keller

Day 28, Patience: *The Compound Effect* - Darren Hardy

Day 29, Guide: *Building a Story Brand* - Donald Miller

Day 30, Fear: *Wild at Heart* - John Eldridge

Day 31, Humility: *Humility, Updated Edition* - Andrew Murray

Contact:

THE IDEAL PROFESSIONAL SPEAKER FOR YOUR NEXT EVENT!

Any organization that wants to develop their people to become "wise beyond their years," is going to want to hire Andrew for a keynote, workshop, or presentation today!

TO CONTACT OR BOOK ANDREW TO SPEAK
(855) ANDREWH (263-7394)
Or
info@andrewahall.com

Keep in touch:

If you want more wisdom in your life and you're sick of the pain your level of thinking has gotten you into, you'll want to sign up for the Wisdom email list. Send Andrew an email with the subject line: "Wisdom email list" and share something you learned from the book.

WisdomBook@AndrewAHall.com

Acknowledgement:

My deepest thanks to my wife, Marissa, my unwavering belief builder and editor, who's shaped my vision since our 2019 adventure began. To Sue Hatley, my elementary science teacher, and countless mentors who said, "Andrew, you're wise beyond your years," your faith ignited this book. Your trust inspires me to guide others.

About the author:

Andrew Hall is a coach, speaker, and conflict resolution expert who helps young leaders and entrepreneurs gain clarity, build confidence, and become wise beyond their years. He lives in Akron, Ohio, with his wife Marissa and their children.